RISING TO THE OCCASION

Paul Dickson

Rising to the Occasion

THE BEST TOASTS FOR ANY CELEBRATION

BLOOMSBURY

NEW YORK • LONDON • NEW DELHI • SYDNEY

Published by Bloomsbury USA, New York

Bloomsbury is a trademark of Bloomsbury Publishing Plc

All papers used by Bloomsbury USA are natural, recyclable products made
from wood grown in well-managed forests. The manufacturing processes
conform to the environmental regulations of the country of origin.

LIBRARY OF CONGRESS CATALOGING-IN-
PUBLICATION DATA HAS BEEN APPLIED FOR

ISBN: 978-1-62040-663-2

First U.S. Edition 2014

3 5 7 9 10 8 6 4 2

Typeset by Hewer Text UK Ltd, Edinburgh
Printed and bound in the U.S.A. by Thomson-Shore Inc., Dexter, Michigan

Bloomsbury books may be purchased for business or promotional use.
For information on bulk purchases please contact Macmillan Corporate
and Premium Sales Department at specialmarkets@macmillan.com.

Contents

The Art of Toasting

A TOAST IS a basic form of human expression that is used to mark special moments and occasions. Toasts can be sentimental, cynical, lyric, comic, defiant, long, short, or even just a single word. Here are some basic rules of thumb if you are called upon to deliver a toast.

1. **PREPARE AHEAD AND KEEP THE TOAST SHORT.** If you haven't prepared, it will most likely run too long. Think it through, write it down, and practice once or twice. Mark Twain said that no toast—other than the ones he gave—should last for more than one minute. So no more than a minute. Most toasts should not exceed thirty seconds.

2. **BE KIND AND SINCERE AND DON'T TRY TO BE FUNNY IF YOU ARE NOT.** What you're really aiming to be is amusing. *Sincerity* and *preparation* are the two key words. Steal from Shakespeare, steal from the Bible, but give it some thought. "One mistake people make at weddings and big events is they try to be funny. If you're going to try and be funny, please, please, please, on behalf of all the people sitting in the audience, test your material in advance on someone who won't lie to you or give you token laughs," Renate Zorn, coordinator of District 60 of the Toastmasters Speakers Bureau, which covers most of southern Ontario, told the *Toronto Star* in a September 2004 article on toasting. "It's for your own good: Anyone who has told a joke to a couple of hundred people and bombed knows that's not an experience worth trying twice. And if you can't make

one person laugh with a line, I guarantee you're not getting a roomful to even crack a smile."

3. THINK OF YOUR TOAST AS A TERRIBLY IMPORTANT VERBAL SOUVENIR. People remember a really good—or really bad—toast long after the event at which it was delivered. The function is to elevate the mood of the room even one notch higher. It's to give everyone the sense of commonality. This is especially true of wedding toasts, but it works for other important occasions from baptisms to retirement parties. People go out and spend two hours renting a tux or buying a gown, but they won't spend any time on the toast, which may be the most important souvenir of the day.

4. STAND AND DELIVER. Always stand when delivering a toast and hold the glass straight from your shoulder in your right hand. Speak clearly and confidently. Make sure that you didn't drink too much previously. You need to be able to speak loud enough for people to hear and clearly so everyone will understand. Introduce yourself briefly, if you aren't already known by everyone present. The fact that the toaster and the guests are holding their glasses hoisted is another reason for brevity. It is also a reason for relative sobriety. If the best man or other functionary has tippled too much champagne before delivering a toast, he can ramble on while the guests' arms fall asleep under the strain of full glasses.

5. END UP. Always end your toast on a positive note and alert the guests to join in. For example, say to the audience, "Cheers!" or "Raise your glass."

6. CLINK BEFORE YOU DRINK. Clink—but do not clunk—your glass after the toast is given, but before you drink. The clinking of glasses goes back to an old belief that the devil is frightened away by bells—church bells and others. It began as a protective gesture which still has a nice ring to it.

7. NEVERS. NEVER refuse to participate in a toast. It is better to toast with an empty glass than not at all.

NEVER use a toast to complain or advance a personal agenda—it ain't about you.

NEVER clank your glass with a spoon—it is disharmonious and can destroy good stemware.

NEVER exclude anyone because they do not have a full glass and always make sure that minors and nondrinkers are provided for. There's nothing worse than cutting out a nine-year-old from a wedding toast because somebody forgot the ginger ale. A toast is the ultimate act of inclusion, so nobody gets left out.

NEVER bring up ex-wives, old boyfriends, academic failure, inside jokes that nobody understands, or try to turn these into something funny.

AND NEVER, NEVER EVER CONFUSE A TOAST WITH A PRACTICAL JOKE. The best man's toast is not a good time for practical joking. Alan Feldman, of Alan Feldman's Photography in Brandon, Florida, has seen that go awry. As he told a reporter for the *Tampa Tribune* in 1996 for an article on toasting disasters, he worked at a wedding in which the best man passed out keys to about thirty women. When the best man raised his glass to toast the newlyweds, he announced it was time for all the women who were having affairs with the groom to return his house keys. The multitudes walked up and dropped the keys in front of the bride.

"She was so upset; it ruined the rest of the wedding," said Feldman adding, "No doubt the honeymoon was heavy on the chill and light on the bubbly." Feldman said the bride did not talk to the groom—presumably because he had chosen such a best man—for the rest of the reception.

8. RULE FOR THE TOASTEE: Respond to the toast appropriately. If you are the toastee (the person being toasted), do not stand or drink to yourself. Once the toast is finished, you may bow or thank in acknowledgment. You may also raise your own glass to propose a toast to the host, the toaster, or anyone else.

TOASTS
FOR EVERY
OCCASION

Toasts

AGE

A man is only as old as the woman he feels.
—GROUCHO MARX

Do not resist growing old—many are denied the privilege.

Fill high the goblet! Envious time steals, as we speak, our fleeting prime.

Here's a health to the future;
A sigh for the past;
We can love and remember,
And hope to the last,
And for all the base lies
That the almanacs hold
While there's love in the heart,
We can never grow old.

Here's hoping that you live forever
And mine is the last voice you hear.
—WILLARD SCOTT, from *A Gentleman's Guide to Toasting*

Here's that we may live to eat the hen
That scratches on our grave.

I've never known a person to live to 110 or more, and then die, to be
remarkable for anything else.
—JOSH BILLINGS

Let him live to be a hundred! We want him on earth.
—OLIVER WENDELL HOLMES to a friend

Long life to you and may you die in your own bed.

May our lives, like the leaves of the maple, grow
More beautiful as they fade.
May we say our farewells, when it's time to go,
All smiling and unafraid.
—LARRY E. JOHNSON

May the Lord love us but not call us too soon.

May virtue and truth
Guide you in youth
Catnip and sage
Cheer your old age.
—Found in a geography book dated 1880, Cuttingsville, Vermont

May we keep a little of the fuel of youth to warm our body in old age.

May you enter heaven late.

May you live as long as you want, may you never want as long as you
live.

8

May you live to be a hundred—and decide the rest for yourself.

Noah was six hundred years old before he knew how to build an ark—don't lose your grip.
—ELBERT HUBBARD

Oh to be seventy again!
—OLIVER WENDELL HOLMES JR. on the occasion of his passing a
   pretty girl on the street at the age of about eighty-five

Only the young die good.
—OLIVER HERFORD

The good die young—here's hoping that you may live to a ripe old age.

To maturity:
When there's snow on the roof,
there's fire in the furnace.

To the Old Guard, the older we grow,
The more we take and the less we know.
At least the young men tell us so,
But the day will come, when they shall know
Exactly how far a glass can go,
To win the battle, 'gainst age, the foe.
Here's youth . . . in a glass of wine.
—JAMES MONROE McLEAN, *The Book of Wine*

To the old, long life and treasure;
To the young, all health and pleasure.
—BEN JONSON

You're not as young as you used to be
But you're not as old as you're going to be
So watch it!
—Irish

ANNIVERSARIES

Here is to loving, to romance, to us.
May we travel together through time.
We alone count as none, but together we're one,
For our partnership puts love to rhyme.
—Irish

Here's to you both—
a beautiful pair,
on the birthday
of your love affair.

Let anniversaries come and let anniversaries go—but may your happiness continue on forever.

Love seems the swiftest, but it is the slowest of growths. No man or woman really knows what perfect love is until they have been married a quarter of a century.
—Mark Twain

May the warmth of our affections survive the frosts of age.

To your coming anniversaries—may they be outnumbered only by your coming pleasures.

We've holidays and holy days, and memory days galore;
And when we've toasted every one, I offer just one more.
So let us lift our glasses high, and drink a silent toast—
The day, deep buried in each heart, that each one loves the most.

With fifty years between you
and your well-kept wedding vow.
The Golden Age, old friends of mine,
is not a fable now.
— "The Golden Wedding at Longwood" by JOHN GREENLEAF WHITTIER

BABIES AND CHILDREN

A baby will make love stronger, days shorter, nights longer, bankroll smaller, home happier, clothes shabbier, the past forgotten, and the future worth living for.

A new life begun,
Like father, like son.
— Irish

A generation of children on the children of your children.

A lovely being scarcely formed or molded,
A rose with all its sweetest leaves yet folded.
— LORD BYRON

Every baby born into the world is a finer one than the last.
— CHARLES DICKENS, *Nicholas Nickleby*

Father of fathers, make me one,
A fit example for a son.
—DOUGLAS MALLOCH'S toast for fathers with a son or sons

Grandchildren are gifts of God.
It is God's way . . .
Of compensating us for growing old.
—Irish

Here's to the baby—man to be—
May he be as fine as thee!
Here's to the baby—woman to be—
May she be as sweet as thee!

Here's to the stork,
A most valuable bird,
That inhabits the residence districts.
He doesn't sing tunes,
Nor yield any plumes,
But he helps the vital statistics.
—Irish

Like one, like the other,
Like daughter, like mother.
—Irish

May he/she grow twice as tall as yourself and half as wise.
—Irish

Out of a love our child will grow . . .
Greater than light, deeper than dark,
All other love is but a spark.

So that our children will have wealthy parents.

The Babies. —As they comfort us in our sorrows, let us not forget them in our festivities.
—MARK TWAIN

"The stork has brought a little peach!"
The nurse said with an air.
"I'm mighty glad," the father said.
"He didn't bring a pear."

[To the new parent(s)]
Trust yourself. You know more than you think you do.
—BENJAMIN SPOCK, U.S. psychologist, advice to a new parent in *Baby and Child Care*, 1977

We haven't all the good fortune to be ladies; we have not all been generals, or poets or statesmen; but when the toast works down to the babies we stand on common ground. We've all been babies.
—MARK TWAIN

BIBLICAL

The Bible does not give us any direct mention of toasting, but there are a number of passages that indicate that the custom was observed. Even an antitoast cleric of the last century had to concede: "It is hardly probable that Ben-hadad and the thirty-two kings, his companions, would drink themselves drunk in the pavilions without some interchange of courtesies" (see 1 Kings 20:16).

A number of lines from the Bible have been used as toasts including these:

A feast is made for laughter, and wine maketh merry.
—Ecclesiastes 10:19

Do not arouse or awaken love until it so desires.
—Song of Solomon 2:7

Drink no longer water, but use a little wine for thy stomach's sake.
—1 Timothy 5:23

Eat thy bread with joy, and drink thy wine with a merry heart.
—Ecclesiastes 9:7

Forsake not an old friend, for the new is not comparable to him. A new friend is as new wine: when it is old, thou shall drink it with pleasure.
—Ecclesiastes 9:10

Give . . . wine unto those that be of heavy heart.
—Proverbs 31:6

The best wine . . . that goeth down sweetly, causing the lips of those that are asleep to speak.
—Song of Solomon 7:9

Wine maketh glad the heart of man.
—Psalms 104:15

Wine nourishes, refreshes, and cheers. Wine is the foremost of all medicines . . . Whenever wine is lacking, medicines become necessary.
—The Talmud

Wine was created from the beginning to make men joyful, and not to make men drunk. Wine drunk with moderation is the joy of the soul and the heart.
—Ecclesiastes 31:35–36

Wine, which cheereth God and man.
—Judges 9:13

BIRTHDAYS

A health, and many of them. Birthdays were never like this when I had 'em.

Although another year is past
He's/She's no older than the last!

Another candle on your cake?
Well, that's no cause to pout,
Be glad that you have strength enough
To blow the damn thing out.

Another year older? Think this way:
Just one day older than yesterday!

God grant you many and happy years,
Till, when the last has crowned you,
The dawn of endless days appears,
And heaven is shining round you!
—Oliver Wendell Holmes

Happy birthday to you
And many to be,
With friends that are true
As you are to me!

Here's to you! No matter how old you are, you don't look it!

Many happy returns of the day of your birth:
Many blessings to brighten your pathway on earth;
Many friendships to cheer and provoke you to mirth;
Many feastings and frolics to add to your girth.
—Robert H. Lord

May you have been born on your lucky star and may that star never
lose its twinkle.

May you live to be a hundred years with one extra year to repent.
—Irish

Time marches on!
Now tell the truth—
Where did you find
The fountain of youth?

To wish you joy on your birthday
And all the whole year through,
For all the best that life can hold
Is none too good for you.

To your birthday, glass held high,
Glad it's you that's older—not I.

CHRISTMAS

A Christmas wish—
May you never forget
what is worth remembering
or remember
what is best forgotten.
—Irish

A Merry Christmas this December
To a lot of folks I don't remember.
—FRANKLIN P. ADAMS, 1922

As fits the holy Christmas birth,
Be this, good friends, our carol still—
Be peace on earth, be peace on earth,
To men of gentle will.
—WILLIAM MAKEPEACE THACKERAY

At Christmas play and make good cheer
For Christmas comes but once a year.
—THOMAS TUSSER

Be merry all, be merry all,
With holly dress the festive hall,
Prepare the song, the feast, the ball,
To welcome Merry Christmas.

Blessed is the season which engages the whole world in a conspiracy
of love.
—HAMILTON WRIGHT MABIE

Christmas is here,
Merry old Christmas,
Gift-bearing, heart-touching, joy-bringing Christmas,
Day of grand memories, king of the year.
—WASHINGTON IRVING

Fifty more Christmases at least in this life, and eternal summers in
another.
—CHARLES DICKENS, Mr. Pickwick's Christmas dinner toast

God bless us every one!
—Tiny Tim's toast, from *A Christmas Carol* by CHARLES DICKENS

Or, for those who would like to savor the entire incident:

At last the dinner was all done, the cloth cleared, the hearth swept, and the fire made up. The compound in the jug being tasted, and considered perfect, apples and oranges were put upon the table, and a shovelful of chestnuts on the fire. Then all the Cratchit family drew around the hearth in what Bob Cratchit called a circle, meaning half a one; and at Bob Cratchit's elbow stood the family display of glass. Two tumblers and a custard-cup without a handle.

These held the hot stuff from the jug, however, as well as golden goblets would have done; and Bob served it out with beaming looks, while the chestnuts on the fire sputtered and crackled noisily. Then Bob proposed:

"A Merry Christmas to us all, my dears. God bless us!"

Which the family re-echoed.

"God bless us every one!" said Tiny Tim, the last of all.

—CHARLES DICKENS, *A Christmas Carol*

Heap on more wood!—the wind is chill
But let it whistle as it will,
We'll keep our Christmas merry still.
—SIR WALTER SCOTT

Here's to the day of good will, cold weather, and warm hearts!

Here's to the holly with its bright red berry.
Here's to Christmas, let's make it merry.

Here's wishing you more happiness
Than all my words can tell,
Not just alone for Christmas
But for all the year as well.

Holly and ivy hanging up
And something wet in every cup.
—Irish

I have always thought of Christmas as a good time; a kind, forgiving, generous, pleasant time; a time when men and women seem by one consent to open their hearts freely; and so I say "God bless Christmas."
—CHARLES DICKENS

I know I've wished you this before
But every year I wish it more,
A Merry Christmas.
—From an old postcard

I wish you a Merry Christmas
And a Happy New Year
A pocket full of money
And a cellar full of beer!

Joy to the world—and especially to you.

May the Virgin and her Child lift your latch on Christmas night.
—Irish. This refers to the old Irish custom of leaving the door unbolted
    and a candle in the window for Mary on her way to Bethlehem.

May you be as contented as Christmas finds you all the year round.
—Irish

May you be poor in misfortune this Christmas
and rich in blessings
slow to make enemies

quick to make friends
and rich or poor, slow or quick,
as happy as the New Year is long.
—Irish

May you be the first house in the parish to welcome St. Nicholas.
—Irish

May you never be without a drop at Christmas.
—Irish

May your corn stand high as yourself, your fields grow bigger with
rain, and the mare know its own way home on Christmas night.
—Irish

May you live as long as you wish, and have all you wish as long as you
live. This is my Christmas wish for you.

May your sheep all have lambs but not on Christmas night.
—Irish

Now, thrice welcome, Christmas!
Which brings us good cheer,
Mince pies and plum pudding,
Strong ale and strong beer!

Peace and plenty for many a Christmas to come.
—Irish

Then here's to the heartening wassail,
Wherever good fellows are found;
Be its master instead of its vassal,

And order the glasses around.
—OGDEN NASH

Then let us be merry and taste the good cheer, and remember old
Christmas comes but once a year.
—From an old Christmas carol

'Twas the month after Christmas,
And Santa had flit;
Came there tidings for father
Which read: "Please remit!"

EXPECTANT PARENTS

Here's to one who born will be,
Born of the body, sowed of the soul,
Born of the flesh of you and me.

Here is the toast of the moon and the stars,
To the child . . . who will soon be ours.

Out of a love our child will grow. . . .
Greater than light, deeper than dark,
All other love is but a spark.

FRIENDSHIP

A day for toil, an hour for sport,
But for a friend life is too short.
—Ralph Waldo Emerson

A health to you,
A wealth to you,
And the best that life can give to you.
May fortune still be kind to you.
And happiness be true to you,
And life be long and good to you,
Is the toast of all your friends to you.

Absent friends—though out of sight we recognize them with our glasses.

Don't walk in front of me,
I may not follow.
Don't walk behind me,
I may not lead.
Walk beside me,
And just be my friend.
—Irish

Friendship: May differences of opinion cement it.

Friendship's the wine of life.
Let's drink of it and to it.

Here's all that's fine to you!
Books and old wine to you!
Girls be divine to you!
—RICHARD HOVEY

Here's to a friend. He knows you well and likes you just the same.

Here's to beefsteak when you're hungry,
Whiskey when you are dry,
Greenbacks when you are busted,
And Heaven when you die!

Here's to cold nights, warm friends, and a good drink to give them.

Here's to eternity—may we spend it in as good company as this night finds us.

Here's to our friendship;
May it be reckoned long as a lifetime,
Close as a second.

Here's to our friends . . . and the strength to put up with them.
—Line used in ads for the movie *The Four Seasons*

Here's to the four hinges of Friendship—
Swearing, Lying, Stealing, and Drinking.
When you swear, swear by your country;
When you lie, lie for a pretty woman;
When you steal, steal away from bad company;
And when you drink, drink with me.

Here's to you, old friend, may you live a thousand years,
Just to sort of cheer things in this vale of human tears;
And may I live a thousand too—a thousand—less a day,
'Cause I wouldn't care to be on Earth and hear you'd passed away.

I drink to the brew of our friendship; it goes to my heart, but never to my head.
—Anonymous

It is around the table that friends understand best the warmth of being together.
—Old Italian saying

I've traveled many a highway
I've walked for many a mile
Here's to the people who made my day
To the people who waved and smiled.
—Tom T. Hall from *A Gentleman's Guide to Toasting*

May the friends of our youth be the companions of our old age.

May the hinges of friendship never rust, nor the wings of love lose a feather.
—DEAN RAMSAY, in *Reminiscences of Scottish Life*

May we have more and more friends, and need them less and less.

May we never have friends who, like shadows, follow us in sunshine only to desert us on a cloudy day.

May your tobacco never run out, your library never turn musty, your cellar never go dry, and your friends never turn foes.

My boat is on the shore,
And my bark is on the sea;
But, before I go, Tom Moore,
Here's a double health to thee.
—LORD BYRON, to Thomas Moore

Never drink anything without first smelling it,
Never sign anything without first reading it.
Never dive into pools of depth unknown,
And rarely drink—if you are alone.
—Seventeenth-century philosophy

Now I, friend, drink to you, friend,
As my friend drank to me,
And I, friend, charge you, friend,
As my friend charged me,
That you, friend, drink to your friend,
As my friend drank to me;

And the more we drink together, friend,
The merrier we'll be!

Old friends are scarce,
New friends are few;
Here's hoping I've found
One of each in you.

Pour deep the rosy wine and drink a toast with me;
Here's to three: Thee, Wine, and Camaraderie!
—THOMAS MOORE

The Lord gives our relatives,
Thank God we can choose our friends.

The world is gay and colorful,
And life itself is new.
And I am very grateful for
The friend I found in you.

Then here's to thee, old friend; and long
May thou and I thus meet,
To brighten still with wine and song
This short life ere it fleet.

To friends: as long as we are able
To lift our glasses from the table.

To my friend. If we ever disagree, may you be in the right.

To our best friends, who know the worst about us but refuse to believe it.

To the spirit of Christmases yet to come.
—World War II toast

We'll think of all the friends we know
And drink to all worth drinking to.

We'll drink the wanting into wealth,
And those that languish into health,
The afflicted into joy,
the oppressed into serenity and rest.
—CHARLES COTTON

Were't the last drop in the well,
As I gasp'd upon the brink,
Ere my fainting spirit fell,
'Tis to thee I would drink.

GENERAL

A handsome new nose to you.

A little health, a little wealth,
A little house and freedom:
With some few friends for certain ends
But little cause to need 'em.

A toast to the wise
And a toast to the foolish
A toast to your eyes—
May they never grow mulish!

Ad multos annos—to many years!
—Latin toast from Governor Mario Cuomo to President Ronald Reagan at
   the 1988 Gridiron dinner, Washington, D.C.

All that gives you pleasure.

All true hearts and sound bottoms.

And fill them high with generous juice,
As generous as your mind,
And pledge me in the generous toast—
The whole of human kind!
—ROBERT BURNS

Be glad of life!
Because it gives you the chance to love and work,
To play and to look up at the stars.
—HENRY VAN DYKE

Be not concerned if thou findest thyself in possession of unexpected
wealth. Allah will provide an unexpected use for it.
—JAMES JEFFREY ROCHE

Blue skies and green lights.

Call frequently,
Drink moderately,
Part friendly,
Pay today
Trust tomorrow.

Days of Ease and Nights of Pleasure.

Delicious nights to every virtuous heart.

Good company, good wine, good welcome make good people.
—SHAKESPEARE, *Henry VIII* Act I

Good day, good health, good cheer, good night!

Health to my body, wealth to my purse,
Heaven to my soul, and I wish you no worse.

Heaven give thee many, many merry days.
—SHAKESPEARE, *Merry Wives of Windsor,* Act V

Here's a toast to all who are here,
No matter where you're from;
May the best day you have seen
Be worse than your worst to come.

Here's hoping how and hoping who
And hoping when and where;
And may all good things come to you
Before you cease to care.

Here's to all of us.
—SIR THOMAS LIPTON

Here's to beauty, wit, and wine, and to a full stomach, a full purse,
and a light heart.

Here's to the 'ealth o' your Royal 'ighness; hand my the skin o' ha goose-
berry be big enough for han humbrella to cover up hall your enemies.
—CADDY'S toast in *Erminie*

Here's to us that are here, to you that are there, and the rest of us everywhere.
—RUDYARD KIPLING

Here's to your good health, and your family's good health, and may you all live long and prosper.
—JOSEPH JEFFERSON, actor, as Rip Van Winkle

Here's tow'ds yer an' tew yer!
'F I never had met yet
I'd never hev knewed yer.

I drink to the days that are.
—WILLIAM MORRIS

I wish thee health,
I wish thee wealth,
I wish thee gold in store,
I wish thee heaven upon earth—
What could I wish thee more?

If you have an appetite for life, stay hungry.

In the garden of life, may your pea pods never be empty.
—BILL COPELAND in the Sarasota, Florida, *Journal*, quoted in *Reader's Digest*, June 1982

It is best to rise from life as from the banquet, neither thirsty nor drunken.
—ARISTOTLE

Love to one, friendship to many, and good will to all.

Make every day a masterpiece.

May life last as long as it is worth wearing.

Make the most of life while you may,
Life is short and wears away!
—WILLIAM OLDYS

May those who deceive us be always deceived.

May our faults be written on the seashore, and every good action prove a wave to wash them out.

May our feast days be many and our fast days be few.
—MARY L. BOOTH

May the clouds in your life form only a background for a lovely sunset.

May the most you wish for be the least you get.

May you have warmth in your igloo, oil in your lamp, and peace in your heart.
—ESKIMO TOAST

May we all live in pleasure and die out of debt.

May we be happy and our enemies know it. May we live respected and die regretted.

May we breakfast with Health, dine with Friendship, crack a bottle with Mirth, and sup with the goddess Contentment.

May we live to learn well, and learn to live well.

May we never do worse.

May we never feel want, nor ever want feeling.

May we never flatter our superiors or insult our inferiors.

May we never know want till relief is at hand.

May you always distinguish between the weeds and the flowers.

May you be merry and lack nothing.
—Shakespeare

May you get it all together before you come apart.
—Bill Leary, quoted in *Reader's Digest*, June 1982

May you have the hindsight to know where you've been . . . the foresight to know where you're going.
—Charles M. Meyer

May you live all the days of your life.
—Jonathan Swift

May you live as long as you want to and want to as long as you live.

May your life be as beautiful as a summer day with just enough clouds to make you appreciate the sunshine.
—Found inscribed in a book and dated 1882

So live that when you come to die, even the undertaker will feel sorry
for you.
—MARK TWAIN

Success to the lover, honor to the brave,
Health to the sick, and freedom to the slave.

The riotous enjoyment of a quiet conscience.

The three generals in power: General Employment, General Industry,
and General Comfort.

There is no satiety
In our society
With the variety
of your *esprit*.
Here's a long purse to you,
And a great thirst to you!
Fate be no worse to you
Than she's been to me!

'Tis hard to tell which is best,
music, food, drink, or rest.

'Tis not so bad a world,
As some would like to make it;
But whether good or whether bad,
Depends on how you take it.

To the old, long life and treasure;
To the young, all health and pleasure;
To the fair, their face,

With eternal grace;
And the rest, to be loved at leisure.
—Ben Jonson

Two ins and one out—in health, wealth, and out of debt.

While we live, let us live.

Wit without virulence, wine without excess, and wisdom without affectation.

You shall and you shan't,
You will and you won't,
You're condemned if you do,
And you are damned if you don't.

GRACES

Be present at our table, Lord.
Be here and everywhere adored.
These mercies bless, and grant that we
May feast in Paradise with Thee.
—John Cennick, 1741

Bless, O Lord, this food to our use, and us to Thy service,
and make us ever needful of the needs of others, in Jesus' name, Amen.
—Traditional Protestant grace

Bless these thy gifts, most gracious God,
From whom all goodness springs;
Make clean our hearts and feed our souls
With good and joyful things.

Bless this food and us that eats it.
—Cowboy grace

Bless us, O Lord, and these Thy gifts which we have received
out of Thy bounty, through Christ Our Lord. Amen.
—Traditional Catholic grace

Bless, O Lord, these delectable vittles;
May they add to your glory,
not to our middles.
—Twentieth-century American grace

Come, Lord Jesus, Be our guest, and let Thy gifts to us be blessed. Amen.

For a' Thou'st placed upon the table, we thank the Lord, as well's
we're able.

For health and strength and daily food,
We praise thy name, O Lord.

For the air we breathe,
and the water we drink,
For a soul and a mind
with which to think,
For food that comes
from fertile sod,
For these, and many things

I'm thankful to my God.

—Thanksgiving grace written by comedian Danny Thomas when he was in
the sixth grade

For rabbits young and rabbits old,
For rabbits hot, and rabbits cold,
For rabbits tender, rabbits tough,
We thank Thee, Lord, we've had enough!

—DEAN JONATHAN SWIFT, who undoubtedly suffered from an endless
round of luncheons in his honor, just as today's celebrities do. But
whereas the modern complaint might be of too much chicken, Swift had
a different lament.

For Thy benefits, O Lord, we give Thee thanks.

—Grace after meat

For what we are about to receive, the Lord make us truly thankful, for
Christ's sake. Amen.

—Old English classic, which is probably the best known of all Christian
English-language graces

Give me a good digestion, Lord,
And also something to digest;
Give me a healthy body, Lord,
And sense to keep it at its best.

—DR. FURSE, bishop of St. Albans

God bless the master of this house,
God bless the mistress too;
And all the little children
Who round the table go.

—Traditional British grace

God is great, God is good,
We will thank Him for this food.
By his hand must all be fed
Thanks be to God for our daily bread.
—Traditional children's grace

Good bread, good meat
Good God, let's eat!

Heavenly father bless us,
And keep us all alive;
There's ten of us for dinner
And not enough for five.

Here a little child I stand
Heaving up my either hand;
Cold as paddocks though they be,
Here I lift them up to Thee,
For a benison to fall
On our meat, and on us all.
Amen.
— ROBERT HERRICK, "ANOTHER GRACE FOR A CHILD"

Lift up your hands toward the sanctuary and bless the Lord. Blessed art Thou, O Lord our God, King of the Universe, who brings forth bread from the earth. Amen.
—Traditional Jewish thanksgiving before meals

Lord God, we thank you for all the good things you provide, and we pray for the time when people everywhere shall have the abundance they need.

May the Lord make us thankful for what we are about to receive, and for what Mr. Jones hath already received. Amen.
—Grace used to rebuke anyone who starts eating too soon

May the good Lord take a liking to you—but not too soon!

May the holy Saints be about your bed, and about your board, from this time to the latter end—God help us all!
—Irish

May the peace and blessing of God
descend upon us as we receive of his bounty,
and may our hearts be filled
with love for one another.

Ma Kettle: "Say grace, Pa."
Pa Kettle (removing his hat, looking up): "Much obliged, Lord."
—From a Ma and Pa Kettle movie in which they are seated at a bountiful table surrounded by their large family.

O Lord above, send us thy grace
to be our stay,
So as we never do that which brings
unto the wicked sinful way,
The wicked sinful way.
—THOMAS WYTHORNE. This grace was sung and is believed to be one used by the Pilgrims on the *Mayflower*.

O Lord, we thank you for the gifts of your bounty
which we enjoy at this table.
As you have provided for us in the past,
so may you sustain us throughout our lives.

While we enjoy your gifts,
may we never forget the needy and those in want.

O thou that blest the loaves and fishes,
Look down upon these two poor dishes,
And tho' the murphies are but small,
O make them large enough for all,
For if they do our bellies fill
I'm sure it is a miracle.
(Murphies are potatoes.)

Praise to God who giveth meat,
Convenient unto all to eat;
Praise for tea and buttered toast
Father, Son, and Holy Ghost.
—Old Scottish grace

Pray for peace and grace and spiritual food,
For wisdom and guidance, for all these are good,
But don't forget the potatoes.
— J. T. PETTEE, "Prayer and Potatoes"

"Pray God bless us all," said jolly Robìn,
"And our meat within this place;
A cup of sack good, to nourish our blood,
And so I do end my grace."
— From "Robin Hood and the Butcher," *The Oxford Book of Ballads*

Some have meat but cannot eat;
Some could eat but have no meat;
We have meat and can all eat;
Blest, therefore, be God for our meat.

— The Selkirk Grace, found in the papers of Dr. Plume of Maldon, Essex
in a handwriting of about 1650

Another version, attributed to Robert Burns, is the one invoked at
traditional Burns Night celebrations. The birthday of Robert Burns,
the well-known Scottish poet, was January 25, and it has become
traditional to gather for a meal on or near this date with haggis as the
main dish. The first Burns Night celebration took place shortly after
his death in 1796. Various toasts—usually made with whiskey—are
proposed during or after the meal which is usually followed by a
program of songs, poems, and dances. Traditionally, the supper
begins with a recitation of the Selkirk Grace and a bowl of broth,
followed by the dramatic arrival of the haggis.

Some hae meat, and canna eat,
And some wad eat that want it
But we hae meat, and we can eat,
And sae the Lord be thankit.

Thank the Lord for what we've gotten,
If ther 'ad been mooar, mooar we shud hev etten.

To God who gives us daily bread
A thankful song we raise,
And pray that he who sends us food
Will fill our hearts with praise.

We thank thee, Father, for thy care
And for thy bounty everywhere;
For this and every other gift,
Our grateful hearts to thee we lift.

What we are about to receive, may the Trinity and Unity bless, Amen.
—Grace before meat

GUESTS

Here's to our guest—
Don't let him rest.
But keep his elbow bending.
'Tis time to drink—
Full time to think
Tomorrow—when you're mending.

May our house always be too small to hold all our friends.
—Myrtle Reed

Our house is ever at your service.

See, your guests approach:
Address yourself to entertain them sprightly,
And let's be red with mirth.
—Shakespeare, *The Winter's Tale*, Act IV

Stay happy, my friend, hang easy and loose
Gettin' rattlesnake-riled is just no use
So here is a slogan that's sure hard to match
There ain't no use itchin' unless you can scratch!
—Cowboy welcome from a sampler

The ornament of a house is the guests who frequent it.

To Our Guest! A friend of our friend's is doubly our friend. Here's to him.

You are welcome here
Be at your ease
Get up when ready
Go to bed when you please.
Happy to share with you
Such as we've got
The leaks in the roof
The soup in the pot.
You don't have to thank us
Or laugh at our jokes
Sit deep and come often
You're one of the folks.
—Notice found in Aspen, Colorado, guesthouse and quoted by Erica
    Wilson in the *Washington Post*, 1980

HALLOWEEN

From ghoulies and ghosties
And long-leggedy beasties
And things that go bump in the night,
Good Lord, deliver us!
—A prayer from Cornwall known as the "Cornish Litany." It was first
    printed in Frederick Thomas Nettleinghame's *Polperro Proverbs and
    Others*, published in 1926 by the Cornish Arts Association, but it's
    certainly much older.

Now it is the time of night
That the graves, all gaping wide,
Every one lets forth his sprite,
In the church-way paths to glide.
—SHAKESPEARE, *A Midsummer Night's Dream*, Act V. The line, uttered
   by Puck, is not specifically referring to Halloween, but the sentiment
   conjures up images of the day.

The evening of October 31 is Hallowe'en or Nut Crack Night. It is
clearly a relic of pagan times but still very popular. It is a night set apart
for walking about and playing harmless pranks, such as placing the hotel
omnibus on top of the Baptist church or plugging the milkman's pump.
—KIN HUBBARD

When black cats prowl and pumpkins gleam,
May luck be yours on Halloween.

HEALTH

Early to rise and early to bed
makes a male healthy and wealthy and dead.
—JAMES THURBER

Here's a health to every one;
Peace on earth, and heaven won.

Here's to your health—a long life and an easy death to you.

Here's to your health! You make age curious, time furious, and all of
us envious.

That a doctor might never earn a dollar out of you—and that your heart may never give out.

The best doctors in the world are Doctor Diet, Doctor Quiet, and Doctor Merryman.
—JONATHAN SWIFT

The health of the salmon to you: a long life, a full heart, and a wet mouth!
—Irish

To your good health, old friend,
may you live for a thousand years,
and I be there to count them.
—ROBERT SMITH SURTEES

HOME

God bless our mortgaged home.

Here's to home, the place where we are treated best, and grumble the most.
—From an old postcard

Long may your lum reek.
—ROBERT BURNS
(Translation: "Long may your chimney smoke.")

May blessings be upon your house,
Your roof and hearth and walls;
May there be lights to welcome you
When evening's shadow falls—
The love that like a guiding star
Still signals when you roam;
A book, a friend—these be the things
That make a house a home.
—MYRTLE REED, a house blessing

HOSTS AND HOSTESSES

A toast to our host
And a song from the short and tall of us,
May he live to be
The guest of all of us!

Here's a health to thine and thee,
not forgetting mine and me.
When thine and thee again meet mine and me,
may mine and me have as much welcome for thine and thee
as thine and thee have had for mine and me tonight.
—Irish

Here's to our hostess, considerate and sweet;
Her wit is endless, but when do we eat?

I thank you for your welcome which was cordial,
And your cordial, which is welcome.

Let's drink to the maker of the feast, our friend and host. May his generous heart, like his good wine, only grow mellower with the years.

May the roof above us never fall in, and may we friends gathered below never fall out.
—Irish

May you be Hung, Drawn, and Quartered!
Yes—Hung with diamonds,
Drawn in a coach and four,
And quartered in the best houses in the land.

To our host,
An excellent man;
For is not a man
Fairly judged by the
Company he keeps?

To the sun that warmed the vineyard,
To the juice that turned to wine,
To the host that cracked the bottle,
And made it yours and mine.

To our hostess! She's a gem. We love her, God bless her.
And the devil take her husband.

To our host: The rapturous, wild, and ineffable pleasure of drinking
at somebody else's expense.
Henry Sambrooke Leigh, 1870

What's a table richly spread
Without a woman at its head?

You are welcome, my fair guests; that noble lady,
Our gentleman, that is not freely merry,
Is not my friend: This to confirm my welcome:
And to you all good health.
—Shakespeare, *Henry VIII*, Act I

HUSBANDS

Here's to the man who loves his wife,
And loves his wife alone.
For many a man loves another man's wife,
When he ought to be loving his own.

May your life be long and sunny
And your husband fat and funny.

To my husband—may he never be tight; but tight or sober, my husband.

When the husband drinks to the wife, all would be well; when the wife drinks to the husband, all is.
—Old English proverb

INTERNATIONAL

An assembly of short toasts or, as they have been called, cheers to get you through a United Nations reception. Their English equivalents are along the lines of Cheers, To your health, and Bottoms up.

ALBANIAN: Gëzuar.

ARABIAN: Bismillah. Fi schettak.

ARMENIAN: Genatzt.

AUSTRIAN: Prosit.

BELGIAN: Op uw gezonheid.

BRAZILIAN: Saúde. Viva.

CHINESE: Nien Nien nu e. Kong Chien. Kan bei. Yum sen. Wen lie.

CZECHOSLOVAKIAN: Na Zdravi. Nazdar.

DANISH: Skål.

DUTCH: Proost. Geluch.

EGYPTIAN: Fee sihetak.

ESPERANTO: Je zia sano.

ESTONIAN: Tervist.

FINNISH: Kippis. Maljanne.

FRENCH: A votre santé. Santé.

GERMAN: Prosit. Auf ihr wohl.

GREEK: Eis Igian.

GREENLANDIC: Kasûgta.

HAWAIIAN: Okole maluna. Hauoli maoli oe. Meli kalikama.

HUNGARIAN: Kedves egeszsegere.

ICELANDIC: Santanka nu.

INDIAN: Jaikind. Aanand.

INDONESIAN: Selamat.

IRANIAN: Besalmati. Shemoh.

ITALIAN: A la salute. Salute. Cin cin.

JAPANESE: Kampai. Banzai.

KOREAN: Kong gang ul wi ha yo.

LITHUANIAN: I sveikas.

MALAYAN: Slamat minum.

MEXICAN: Salud.

MOROCCAN: Saha wa'afiab.

NEW ZEALAND: Kia ora.

NORWEGIAN: Skål.

PAKISTANI: Sanda bashi.

PHILIPPINE: Mabuhay.

POLISH: Na zdrowie. Vivat.

PORTUGUESE: A sua saúde.

ROMANIAN: Noroc. Pentru sanatatea dunneavoastra.

RUSSIAN: Na zdorovia.

SPANISH: Salud. Salud, amor y pesetas y el tiempo para gustarlos! (Health, love, and money and the time to enjoy them!)

SWEDISH: Skål.

THAI: Sawasdi.

TURKISH: Şerefe.

UKRAINIAN: Boovatje zdorovi.

WELSH: Iechyd da.

YUGOSLAVIAN: Zivio.

ZULU: Oogy wawa.

IRISH

There is no area of the world where English is spoken—and probably none where any other language is spoken for that matter—that can compare to Ireland as a stronghold for the custom of toasting. More often than not, toasts go by the name of "blessings" in Ireland. There are large numbers of them, and their use seems to be growing. John B. Keane said in a recent article on the subject, "Nothing has the grace or the beauty of an old Irish blessing and recently I was delighted to learn that instead of dying out, Irish blessings are on the increase. All you have to do is listen and if you spend a day in the Irish countryside you will go away with countless blessings ringing in your ears."

Blessings are often used beyond the reach of a glass, but all make appropriate toasts. A graveside blessing—"That the devil mightn't hear of his death till he's safe inside the walls of heaven"—can be equally appropriate as a toast to the departed.

The vast majority of toasts in this section (along with others scattered throughout the rest of the book) come from the collection of Jack McGowan of the Irish Distillers International of Dublin, who has pulled them together from all over his nation.

One other thing: Many Irish toasts are one-liners that lend themselves to being assembled into longer toasts. This is especially true of the many *May you's*.

A goose in your garden except on Christmas Day.

Better be quarreling than lonesome.
–Irish Proverb

Health and long life to you.
The wife/husband of your choice to you.
A child every year to you.

Land without rent to you.
And may you be half an hour in heaven
before the devil knows you're dead.
Sláinte! (Pronounced *slawn-cheh;* it means Health!)

Health and long life to you
The wife of your choice to you
Land free of rent to you
From this day forth.

Health to Everyone
From the tip of the roof to the side of the fire
From wall to wall
And if there's anyone *in* the wall, speak up!

Here's a health to your enemies' enemies!

Here's that ye may never die nor be kilt till ye break your bones over a bushel of glory.

Here's to_____.When God measures you, may he put the tape around your big and generous heart and not around your small and foolish head.

Here's to a fair price on a fair day.

Here's to eyes in your head and none in your spuds!

Here's to health, peace, and prosperity;
May the flower of love never be nipped by the frost of disappointment; nor shadow of grief fall among a member of this circle.

Here's to the land of the shamrock so green,
Here's to each lad and his darling colleen,
Here's to the ones we love dearest and most,
And may God save old Ireland—that's an Irishman's toast.

Here's to your health
May God bring you luck
And may your journey be smooth and happy.

It is not a sin not to be Irish, but it is a great shame.
—SEAN O'HUIGINN, former consul general of Ireland

May meat always sweeten your pot.

May the day keep fine for you.

May the devil say a prayer for you.

May the enemies of Ireland never meet a friend.

May the frost never afflict your spuds.
May the outside leaves of your cabbage always be free from worms.
May the crows never pick your haystack and may your
donkey always be in foal.

May the horns of your cattle touch heaven.

May the path to hell grow green for lack of travelers.

May the road rise to meet you.
May the wind be always at your back,
the sun shine warm upon your face,

the rain fall soft upon your fields,
and until we meet again
may God hold you in the hollow of His hand.

May the rocks in your field turn to gold.

May the saints protect you,
And sorrow neglect you,
And bad luck to the one
That doesn't respect you.

May the ship that took your sons away
to farm the Californias
bring home a harvest of riches for Christmas.

May the swallows be first in your eaves.
May your milk never turn.
May your horses never stray.
May your hens always lay.
May lean bacon hang from your rafters.

May the thatch on your house
be as strong as the thatch on your head;
May the moon be as full as your glass
and American dollars arrive in the post by Christmas.

May there always be work for your hands to do.
May your purse always hold a coin or two.
May the sun always shine on your windowpane.
May a rainbow be certain to follow each rain.
May the hand of a friend always be near you.
May God fill your heart with gladness to cheer you.

May those who love us love us;
And those that don't love us,
May God turn their hearts;
And if He doesn't turn their hearts,
May He turn their ankles,
So we'll know them by their limping.

May what goes down not come back up again.

May you always wear silk.

May you be seven times better off a year from now.

May you die in bed at ninety-five years, shot by a jealous husband/wife.

[For the bachelor]
May you have nicer legs than yours under the table before the new spuds are up.

May you have the hindsight to know where you've been, the foresight to know where you're going, and the insight to know when you're going too far.

May you have warm words on a cold evening,
A full moon on a dark night,
And the road downhill all the way to your door.

May you look back on the past with as much pleasure as you look forward to the future.

May you never give cherries to pigs or advice to a fool nor praise the green corn till you've seen the ripe field.

May you never have to eat your hat.

May you never make an enemy
when you could make a friend
unless you meet a fox among your chickens.

May your blessings outnumber
the shamrocks that grow,
And may trouble avoid you
wherever you go.

May your fire be as warm as the weather is cold.

May your fire never go out.

May your shadow never grow less.

May your well never run dry.

No wasps near your honey, but bees in your hive.

That the ten toes of your feet might always steer you
clear of misfortune, and I hope,
before you're much older,
that you'll hear much better toasts than this.
Sláinte!

The Irish heart—quick and strong in its generous impulses,
firm in its attachments, sound to the core.

To a full moon on a dark night
And the road downhill all the way to your door.

To a warm bed, a dry stook, and glass in your window.
(A stook is a sheaf of grain.)

To the thirst that is yet to come.

To the three skills of a hare
sharp turning,
high jumping,
and strong running against the hill.

To twenty years a growing
twenty years at rest
twenty years declining
and twenty years when it doesn't matter
whether we're there or not.

To warm words on a cold day.

Wert thou all that I wish thee,
Great, glorious and free,
First flower of the earth,
And first gem of the sea.
—Thomas Moore

Your Health! May we have one together in ten years time
and a few in between.

JEWISH

The prime Jewish toast is the Hebrew *L'chayim*, which means "to life," or "to your health." *Mazel tov* is also used as a toast. Leo Rosten explains which to use when in his *Joys of Yiddish*: "Some innocents confuse *L'chayim* with *mazel tov*, using one when the other would be appropriate. There is no reason to err. *L'chayim* is used whenever one would say 'Your health,' 'Cheers!' or (I shudder to say) 'Here's mud in your eye.' *Mazel tov!* is used as 'Congratulations.'"

LOVE

A Book of Verses underneath the Bough,
A Jug of Wine, a Loaf of Bread—and Thou
Beside me singing in the Wilderness—
Oh, Wilderness were Paradise enow!
—EDWARD FITZGERALD, from *The Rubáiyát of Omar Khayyám*

Because I love you truly,
Because you love me, too,
My very greatest happiness
Is sharing life with you.

Brew me a cup for a winter's night.
For the wind howls loud and the furies fight;

Spice it with love and stir it with care,
And I'll toast your bright eyes, my sweetheart fair.
—Minna Thomas Antrim

Come in the evening, or come in the morning,
Come when you are looked for, or come without warning,
A thousand welcomes you will find here before you,
And the oftener you come here, the more I'll adore you.
—Irish

Come live with me, and be my love,
And we will all the pleasures prove,
That valleys, groves, or hills, or fields,
Or woods and steepy mountains yield.
—Christopher Marlowe, "Passionate Shepherd to His Love"

Do you love me
Or do you not?
You told me once
But I forgot.

Give me a kisse, and to that kisse a score;
Then to that twenty, adde a hundred more;
A thousand to that hundred; so kiss on,
To make that thousand up a million;
Treble that million, and when that is done,
Let's kisse afresh, as when we first begun.
—ROBERT HERRICK, from *Hesperides*

Here's to Dan Cupid, the little squirt,
He's lost his pants, he's lost his shirt,
He's lost most everything but his aim,
Which shows that love is a losing game.

Here's to fertility—the toast of agriculture and the bane of love.

Here's to love and unity,
Dark corners and opportunity.

Here's to Love, that begins with a fever and ends with a yawn.

Here's to love—with its billet-doux, bills and coos, biliousness, bills,
and bills of divorcement.

Here's to one and only one,
And may that one be he
Who loves but one and only one,

And may that one be me.

Here's to the land we love and the love we land.

Here's to the maid who is thrifty,
And knows it is folly to yearn,
And picks out a lover of fifty,
Because he has money to burn.

Here's to the pictures on my desk. May they never meet.

Here's to the prettiest, here's to the wittiest,
Here's to the truest of all who are true,
Here's to the neatest one, here's to the sweetest one,
Here's to them all in one—here's to you.

Here's to the wings of love—
May they never molt a feather;

Till my big boots and your little shoes
Are under the bed together.

Here's to the woman that I love
And here's to the woman that loves me,
And here's to all those that love her that I love,
And to those that love her that love me.

Here's to this water,
Wishing it were wine
Here's to you, my darling,
Wishing you were mine.

Here's to those who love us,
And here's to those who don't,
A smile for those who are willing to,
And a tear for those who won't.

Here's to those who'd love us
If we only cared;
Here's to those we'd love,
If we only dared.

Here's to you,
May you live as long as you want to,
May you want to as long as you live.

Here's to you who halves my sorrows and doubles my joys.

I drink to your charm, your beauty and your brains—which gives
you a rough idea of how hard up I am for a drink.
—GROUCHO MARX

I have known many,
liked a few,
Loved one—
Here's to you!

I love you more than yesterday, less than tomorrow.

I would be friends with you and have your love.

If I were I, and you were you, would you?
There are times I would and times I wouldn't,
Times that I could and times I couldn't;

But the times I could and would and I felt game
Are the times I'm with you, dear.

If we cannot love unconditionally, love is already in a critical condition.
—JOHANN WOLFGANG VON GOETHE

It warms me, it charms me,
To mention but her name,
It heats me, it beats me,
And sets me a' on flame.
—ROBERT BURNS

Let us be gay while we may
And seize love with laughter
I'll be true as long as you
But not for a moment after.

Let's drink to love,
Which is nothing—
Unless it's divided by two.

Love, and you shall be loved. All love is mathematically just, as much as the two sides of an algebraic equation.
—RALPH WALDO EMERSON

Love doesn't make the world go 'round. Love is what makes the ride worthwhile.
—FRANKLIN P. JONES

Love is what you've been through with somebody.
—JAMES THURBER

Love makes time pass—
Time makes love pass.

May love draw the curtain and friendship the cork.

May those now love
Who never loved before.
May those who've loved
Now love the more.

May we kiss those we please
And please those we kiss.

May we love as long as we live, and live as long as we love.

Mutual love, the crown of bliss.
—JOHN MILTON

Mystery and disappointment are not absolutely indispensable to the growth of love, but they are often very powerful auxiliaries.
—CHARLES DICKENS, *Nicholas Nickleby*

Say it with flowers
Say it with eats,
Say it with kisses,
Say it with sweets,
Say it with jewelry,
Say it with drink,
But always be careful
Not to say it with ink.

Thou hast no faults, or I no faults can spy;
Thou art all beauty, or all blindness I.

To each man's best and truest love—unless it be himself.

To every lovely lady bright,
I wish a gallant faithful knight;
To every faithful lover, too,
I wish a trusting lady true.
—SIR WALTER SCOTT

The love you give away is the only love you keep.
—ELBERT HUBBARD

They say there's microbes in a kiss,
This rumor is most rife,
Come lady dear, and make of me an invalid for life.

We'll drink to love, love, the one irresistible force that annihilates distance, caste, prejudice, and principles. Love, the pastime of the Occident, the passion of the East. Love, that stealeth upon us like a thief in the night, robbing us of rest, but bestowing in its place a gift more precious than the sweetest sleep. Love is the burden of my toast—here's looking at you.

Were't the last drop in the well,
As I gasped upon the brink,
Ere my fainting spirit fell,
'Tis to thee I would drink.
—LORD BYRON

Yesterday's yesterday while to-day's here,
To-day is to-day till to-morrow appear;
To-morrow's to-morrow until to-day's past—
And kisses are kisses as long as they last.
—OLIVER HERFORD

MAN AND MEN

Here's to man—he is like a coal-oil lamp; he is not especially bright; he is often turned down; he generally smokes; and he frequently goes out at night.

Here's to that most provoking man
The man of wisdom deep
Who never talks when he takes his rest
But only smiles in his sleep.

Here's to the man that kisses his wife
And kisses his wife alone.
For there's many a man kisses another man's wife
When he ought to be kissing his own.
And here's to the man who kisses his child
And kisses his child alone.
For there's many a man kisses another man's child
When he thinks he is kissing his own.

Here's to you, mister,
Whoever you may be.
For you're just the man of the evening,
And nothing more to me.

But, if you and your liquor should conquer,
And I fail to stand the test;
Well, here's to your technique, mister,
I hope it's better than the rest.

I'll drink to the gentleman who I think
Is most entitled to it;
For if anyone ever can drive me to drink
He certainly can do it.

Man is somewhat like a sausage,
Very smooth upon the skin;
But you can never tell exactly
How much hog there is within.

Man is the only animal that laughs, drinks when he is not thirsty, and
makes love at all seasons of the year.
—VOLTAIRE

Men are like candles,
They gleam and are bright,
Men are like candles,
They shine best at night,
Men are like candles,
They sputter about,
And when they are needed
The darn things go out.
—*Charlie Jones' Laughbook,* May 1952

Oh, here's to the good, and the bad men, too
For without them saints would have nothing to do!
Oh, I love them both, and I love them well,

But which I love better, I can never tell.

One must not become attached to animals: they do not last long enough. Or to men: they last too long.

The man we love: He who thinks most good and speaks less ill of his neighbor.

The men that women marry,
And why they marry them, will always be
A marvel and a mystery to the world.
—HENRY WADSWORTH LONGFELLOW

There is more felicity on the far side of baldness than young men can possibly imagine.
—LOGAN PEARSALL SMITH

To the men I've loved
To the men I've kissed
My heartfelt apologies
To the men I've missed!

To Man: He is mad; he cannot make a worm, and yet he will be making gods by dozens.
—MONTAIGNE

Women's faults are many,
Men have only two—
Everything they say,
And everything they do.

NEW YEAR'S

A song for the old, while its knell is tolled,
And its parting moments fly!
But a song and a cheer for the glad New Year,
While we watch the old year die!
—George Cooper

Another year is dawning! Let it be
For better or for worse, another year with thee.

As we start the New Year,
Let's get down on our knees
to thank God we're on our feet.
—Irish

Be at war with your voices, at peace with your neighbors, and let every new year find you a better man.
—BENJAMIN FRANKLIN

Here's to the bright New Year
And a fond farewell to the old;
Here's to the things that are yet to come
And to the memories that we hold.

Here's to you a New Year's toast
May your joy ne'er see a sorrow's ghost.

In the New Year,
may your right hand always be stretched out in friendship,
but never in want.
—Irish

In the year ahead,
May we treat our friends with kindness
and our enemies with generosity.

Let us resolve to do the best we can with what we've got.
—WILLIAM FEATHER

May all your troubles during the coming year be as short as your New Year's resolutions.

May it be the best year yet for you, and everything prosper you may do.

May the best of this year be the worst of next.

May the Lord keep you in his hand and never close his fist too tight on you. And may the face of every good news and the back of every bad news be toward us in the New Year.
—Irish

May the New Year help to make us old.

May the New Year bring summer in its wake.
—Irish

May the New Year grant you
the eye of a blacksmith on a nail
the good humor of a girl at a dance
the strong hand of a priest on his parish.
—Irish

May this sweetest old-time greeting
Heavily laden with good cheers
Bring content, and peace and plenty
Enough to last through all the year.

May your nets be always full—
your pockets never empty.
May your horse not cast a shoe
nor the devil look at you
in the coming year.
—Irish

The Old Man's dead. He was okay, maybe
But here's a health to the brand-new baby.
I give you 20___.

New Year's Resolution:

Ring out the old, ring in the new,
Ring happy bells across the snow;
The year is going, let him go.
—ALFRED LORD TENNYSON

Should auld acquaintance be forgot,
And never brought to min',
Should auld acquaintance be forgot
And days of auld lang syne.
For auld lang syne, my dear,
For auld lang syne,
We'll tak' a cup o' kindness yet,
For auld lang syne.

And here's a hand, my trusty fierce,
And gie's a hand o' thine,
And we'll tak' a right guid willie-waught,
For auld lang syne.
For auld lang syne, my dear,
For auld lang syne,
We'll tak' a cup o' kindness yet,
For auld lang syne.

And surely ye'll be your pint stowpt,
And surely I'll be mine,

And we'll tak' a cup o' kindness yet,
For auld lang syne.
For auld lang syne, my dear,
For auld lang syne,
We'll tak' a cup o' kindness yet,
For auld lang syne.
—ROBERT BURNS

Stir the eggnog, lift the toddy,
Happy New Year, everybody.
—PHYLLIS MCGINLEY

The New Year is ringing in,
May he be bringing in
The good times we've waited for so long in vain!
Without the demanding
All rise and drink standing,
And so say we all of us again and again.

To a firm hand for a flighty beast
an old dog for the long road
a kettle of fish for Friday
and a welcome for the New Year.
—Irish

Welcome be ye that are here,
Welcome all, and make good cheer,
Welcome all, another year.

Whatever you resolve to do,
On any New Year's Day,

Resolve to yourself to be true
And live—the same old way.

PARENTS

Father. May the love and respect we express toward him make up, at least in part, for the worry and care we have visited upon him.

He didn't tell me how to live;
he lived,
and let me watch him do it.
—Clarence Budington Kelland

Here's to the happiest hours of my life—
Spent in the arms of another man's wife;
My mother!

To Life. The first half is ruined by our parents and the second half by our children.

To Mother and Dad on their wedding anniversary:
We never know the love of our parents
for us till we have become parents.
—Henry Ward Beecher

To Mother—may she live long enough to forget what fiends we used to be.

You may have a friend,
you may have a lover,

but don't forget,
your best friend is your mother.
—Traditional autograph album inscription

REUNIONS

Here's a health in homely rhyme
To our oldest classmate, Father Time;
May our last survivor live to be
As bold and wise and as thorough as he!
—Oliver Wendell Holmes

Here's to all of us!
For there's so much good in the worst of us
And so much bad in the best of us,
That it hardly behooves any of us,
To talk about the rest of us.

Some among many gather again,
A glass to their happiness; friendship,
Amen . . .
The Survivors.
—James Monroe McLean, *The Book of Wine*

Then fill the cup, fill high! fill high!
Let joy our goblets crown,
We'll bung Misfortune's scowling eye,
And knock Foreboding down.
—James Russell Lowell, from "To the Class of '38"

To friends: As long as we are able
To lift our glasses from the table.

To the good old days . . . we weren't so good, 'cause we weren't so old!

ST. PATRICK'S DAY

May the Irish hills caress you.
May her lakes and rivers bless you.
May the luck of the Irish enfold you.
May the blessings of St. Patrick behold you.

May the leprechauns be near you to spread luck along your
way and may all the Irish angels smile upon you on St. Pat's Day.

On St. Patrick's Day you should spend time with saints and scholars,
so you know I have two more stops to make.
—St. Patrick's Day toast delivered by Ronald Reagan to Speaker Jim
   Wright on Capitol Hill, 1988

Saint Patrick was a gentleman,
Who, through strategy and stealth,
Drove all the snakes from Ireland—
Here's a bumper to his health.
But not too many bumpers,
Lest we lose ourselves, and then
Forget the good Saint Patrick,
And see the snakes again.

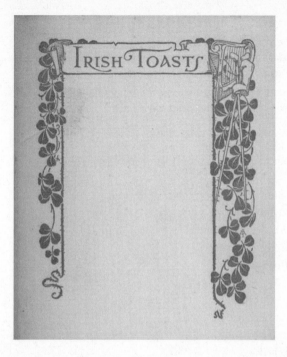

IRISH TOASTS

Success attend St. Patrick's fist,
For he's a saint so clever;
Oh! he give the snakes and toads a twist,
He banished them forever.

The anniversary of St. Patrick's day—and may the shamrock be green forever.

TEMPERANCE

A fig then for Burgundy, Claret or Mountain,
A few scanty glasses must limit your wish.
But here's to the toper that goes to the fountain,
The drinker that verily "drinks like a fish."
—Thomas Hood

Bacchus has drowned more men than Neptune.

Balm of my cares, sweet solace of my toils!
Hail just benignant!
To the unknown beloved
This is my good wishes.
—Coffee toast

Black as the devil,
Strong as death,
Sweet as love, and
Hot as hell!
—Coffee toast

Cold water: We never want cash to buy it, we are never ashamed to ask for it, and never blush to drink it.

Drinking water neither makes a man sick, nor in debt, nor his wife a widow.

He believes in drinking quantities of water
Undiluted by the essence of the grape.
—Harry Graham

Here's to wine—safer outside than in.

I have found water everywhere that I have traveled.
—THOMAS COOK, founder of the international tour company

If you drink like a fish,
Drink what a fish drinks.

Lips that touch wine jelly
Will never touch mine, Nellie.

O' Water for me! Bright Water for me,
And wine for the tremulous debauchee.
—*McGuffey's New Eclectic Speaker*, 1858

Our drink shall be water, bring, sparkling with glee
The gift of our God, and the drink of the free.

There is a devil in every berry of the grape.
—Koran

Water—ever bracing, ever satisfying, ever plenty, and never mocking.

Our National Birds.
The American Eagle   The Thanksgiving Turkey

"May one give us peace in all our states,
The other a piece for all our plates."
E. H. W.

THANKSGIVING

Ah! On Thanksgiving day . . .
When the care-wearied man seeks his mother once more,
And the worn matron smiles where the girl smiled before.
What moistens the lips and what brightens the eye?
What calls back the past, like the rich pumpkin pie?
  —JOHN GREENLEAF WHITTIER

As we express our gratitude, we must never forget that the highest appreciation is not to utter words,
but to live by them.
—JOHN FITZGERALD KENNEDY

Bless, O Lord
These delectable vittles,
May they add to the glory

And not to our middles.
—Yvonne Wright, quoted as a "Thanksgiving Prayer" in the 1986
Reader's Digest, calendar

For turkey braised, the Lord be praised.

God gave you a gift of 86,400 seconds today. Have you used one to say "thank you"?
—William A. Ward

Here's to the blessings of the year,
Here's to the friends we hold so dear,
To peace on earth, both far and near.

Here's to the day when the Yankees first acknowledged Heaven's good gifts with Thank'ees.

Here's to the good old turkey
The bird that comes each fall
And with his sweet persuasive meat
Makes gobblers of us all.

May our pleasures be boundless while we have time to enjoy them.

O Thou who has given us so much, mercifully grant us one thing more—a grateful heart.
—George Herbert

Remember God's bounty in the year. String the pearls of His favor. Hide the dark parts, except so far as they are breaking out in light! Give this one day to thanks, to joy, to gratitude!
—Henry Ward Beecher

Thanksgiving dinners take eighteen hours to prepare. They are consumed in twelve minutes. Half-times take twelve minutes. This is not coincidence.
—ERMA BOMBECK

Thanksgiving Day is a jewel, to set in the hearts of honest men; but be careful that you do not take the day, and leave out the gratitude.
—E. P. POWELL

There is one day that is ours. There is one day when all we Americans who are not self-made go back to the old home to eat saleratus biscuits and marvel how much nearer to the porch the old pump looks than it used to. Thanksgiving Day is the one day that is purely American.
—O. HENRY

To our national birds—
The American eagle,
The Thanksgiving turkey:
May one give us peace in all our States—
And the other a piece for all our plates.

When turkey's on the table laid,
And good things I may scan,
I'm thankful that I wasn't made
A vegetarian.
—EDGAR A. GUEST

WEDDINGS

Weddings require toasts, and best men and other participants are always on the prowl for good raw material to mix into a longer personalized toast. "Health and happiness" and "May all your troubles be little ones" are the most common wedding toasts. They have become cliché.

Some other options:

A Second Marriage: To the triumph of hope over experience.
—SAMUEL JOHNSON, 1770

A toast to love and laughter and happily ever after.

A toast to the groom—and discretion to his bachelor friends.

Down the hatch, to a striking match!

Drink, my buddies, drink with discerning,
Wedlock's a lane where there is no turning;
Never was owl more blind than lover;
Drink and be merry, lads; and think it over.
—Bachelor party toast

Grow old with me!
The best is yet to be,
The last of life,
For which, the first is made.
—ROBERT BROWNING

Here's to my mother-in-law's daughter,
Here's to her father-in-law's son;

And here's to the vows we've just taken,
And the life we've just begun.

Here's to the bride and mother-in-law,
Here's to the groom and father-in-law,
Here's to sister and brother-in-law,
Here's to friends and friends-in-law,
May none of them need an attorney-at-law.

Here's to thee and thy folks from me and my folks;
And if thee and they folks love me and my folks
As much as me and my folks love thee and thy folks,
Then there never was folks since folks was folks
Loved me and my folks as much as thee and thy folks.

Here's to the bride and the groom!
May you have a happy honeymoon,
May you lead a happy life,
May you have a bunch of money soon,
And live without all strife.

Here's to the bride that is to be,
Here's to the groom she'll wed,
May all their troubles be light as bubbles
Or the feathers that make up their bed!

Here's to the groom with bride so fair,
And here's to the bride with groom so rare!

Here's to the happy man: All the world loves a lover.
—RALPH WALDO EMERSON

Here's to the husband—and here's to the wife;
May they remain lovers for life.

I drink to myself and one other,
And may that one other be he
Who drinks to himself and one other,
and may that one other be me.

It is written:
"When children find true love,
parents find true joy."
Here's to your joy and ours,
from this day forward.
—Parents' toast

Let us toast the health of the bride;
Let us toast the health of the groom,
Let us toast the person that tied;
Let us toast every guest in the room.

Look down you gods,
And on this couple drop a blessed crown.
—SHAKESPEARE, *The Tempest*, Act 5

Love, be true to her; Life, be dear to her;
Health, stay close to her; Joy, draw near to her;
Fortune, find what you can do for her,
Search your treasure-house through and through for her,
Follow her footsteps the wide world over—
And keep her husband always her lover.
—ANNA LEWIS, "To the Bride"

Marriage: A community consisting of a master, a mistress, and two slaves—making in all, two.
—AMBROSE BIERCE

Marriage has teeth, and him bit very hot.
—JAMAICAN PROVERB

Marriage is a wonderful institution, but who wants to live in an institution?
—GROUCHO MARX

May their joys be as bright as the morning, and their sorrows but shadows that fade in the sunlight of love.

May their joys be as deep as the ocean
And their misfortunes as light as the foam.

May we all live to be present at their golden wedding.

May you both live as long as you want to, and want to as long as you live.
—LETITIA BALDRIDGE

May you grow old on one pillow.
—Armenian

May you have many children
and may they grow as mature in taste
and healthy in color
and as sought after
as the contents of this glass.
—Irish

May you live forever, may I never die.

May your love be as endless as your wedding rings.

May your wedding days be few and your anniversaries many.

May you have enough happiness to keep you sweet; enough trials to keep you strong; enough sorrow to keep you human; enough hope to keep you happy; enough failure to keep you humble; enough success to keep you eager; enough friends to give you comfort; enough faith and courage in yourself, your business, and your country to banish depression; enough wealth to meet your needs; enough determination to make each day a better day than yesterday.

Needles and pins, needles and pins
When a man marries his trouble begins.

Never above you. Never below you. Always beside you.
—WALTER WINCHELL

Of all life's ceremonies that of marriage is the most touching and beautiful. This is the long anticipated climax of girlhood—and boyhood, too—the doorway to true maturity, the farewell to parents as protectors, the acceptance of responsibility.
—AMY VANDERBILT *Amy Vanderbilt's Etiquette*, 1971

The greatest of all arts is the art of living together.
—WILLIAM LYON PHELPS

There is nothing nobler or more admirable than when two people who see eye to eye keep house as man and wife, confounding their enemies and delighting their friends.
—HOMER, *Odyssey*

These two, now standing hand in hand,
Remind us of our native land,
For when today they linked their fates,
They entered the United States.

To my wife, my bride and joy.

To the newlyweds: May "for better or worse" be far better than worse.

Wedlock's like wine—not properly judged of till the second glass.
—ERNEST JARROLD

With this toast the wish is given
From my graying wife and me,
That you'll be as happily married
As we thought that we would be.
—WILLIAM COLE, 1989, who contributed this original toast for this
    book. He called it "a mean one."

Women often weep at weddings, whereas my own instinct is to laugh uproariously and encourage the bride and groom with merry whoops. The sight of people getting married exhilarates me; I think that they are doing a fine thing, and I admire them for it.
—ROBERTSON DAVIES, "Of Nuptial Merriment," *The Table Talk of
    Samuel Marchbanks*, 1949

You don't marry one person; you marry three—the person you think they are, the person they are, and the person they are going to become as the result of being married to you.
—RICHARD NEEDHAM, *You and All the Rest*, quoted in *Reader's Digest*,
    December 1983

You only get married for the second time once.
—GARRISON KEILLOR, quoted in *Forbes*, November 2, 1987

WINE

A bottle of good wine, like a good act, shines ever in the retrospect.
—ROBERT LOUIS STEVENSON, "The Silverado Squatters"

A warm toast.
Good company.
A fine wine.
May you enjoy all three.

Any port in a storm.

Balm of my cares, sweet solace of my toils, Hail justice benignant!
—THOMAS WHARTON

Clean glasses and old corks.

Comrades, pour the wine tonight
For the parting is with dawn;
Oh, the clink of cups together,
With the daylight coming on!
—RICHARD HOVEY

Count not the cups; not therein lies excess in wine, but in the nature
of the drinker.

Drink wine, and live here blitheful while ye may;
The morrow's life too late is—live today!

For of all labors, none transcend
The works that on the brain depend;
Nor could we finish great designs
Without the power of generous wines.

Give of your wine to others,
Take of their wine to you.
Toast to life, and be toasted awhile,
That, and the cask is through.
—JAMES MONROE MCLEAN, *The Book of Wine*

God, in His goodness, sent the grapes
To cheer both great and small;
Little fools will drink too much,
And great fools none at all.

God made Man,
Frail as a Bubble
God made Love
Love made Trouble
God made the Vine
Was it a sin
That Man made Wine
To drown Trouble in?
—OLIVER HERFORD, *The Deb's Dictionary*

Good wine makes good blood;
Good blood causeth good humors;
Good humors cause good thoughts;

Good thoughts bring forth good works;
Good works carry a man to heaven.
Ergo:
Good wine carrieth a man to heaven.
—JAMES HOWELL, to Lord Clifford, early seventeenth century

He that drinks is immortal
For wine still supplies
What age wears away;
How can he be dust
That moistens his clay?
—HENRY PURCELL

He who clinks his cup with mine,
Adds a glory to the wine.
—GEORGE STERLING

Here's a bumper of wine; fill thine, fill mine:
Here's a health to old Noah, who planted the vine!
—R. H. BARHAM

Here's to mine and here's to thine!
Now's the time to clink it!
Here's a flagon of old wine,
And here we are to drink it.
—RICHARD HOVEY

Here's to old Adam's crystal ale,
Clear, sparkling and divine,
Fair H_2O, long may you flow,
We drink your health (in wine).
—OLIVER HERFORD

Here's to the man who knows enough
To know he's better without the stuff;
Himself without, the wine within,
So come, me hearties, let's begin.

Here's to the man
Who owns the land
That bears the grapes
That makes the wine
That tastes as good
As this does.

Here's to water, water divine—
It dews the grapes that give us wine.

I often wonder what the vintners buy
One half so precious as the stuff they sell.
—OMAR KHAYYÁM

Let those who drink not, but austerely dine, dry up in law; the Muses
smell of wine.
—HORACE

Then a smile, and a glass, and a toast and a cheer,
For all the good wine, and we've some of it here.
—OLIVER WENDELL HOLMES

This bottle's the sun of our table,
His beams are rosy wine;
We, plants that are not able
Without his help to shine.
This wine is full of gases

Which are to me offensive,
It pleases all you asses
Because it is expensive.
—A. P. HERBERT

This wine is too good for toast-drinking, my dear. You don't want to mix emotions up with a wine like that. You lose the taste.
—ERNEST HEMINGWAY, Count Mippipopolous to Brett, in *The Sun Also Rises*

To the big-bellied bottle.

When I die—the day be far!
Should the potters make a jar
Out of this poor clay of mine,
Let the jar be filled with wine!

When wine enlivens the heart
May friendship surround the table.

Wine and women—May we always have a taste for both.

Who was it, I pray,
On the wedding day
Of the Galilean's daughter
With a touch divine
Turned in wine
Six buckets of *filtered* water?
—OLIVER WENDELL HOLMES

Wine improves with age—I like it more the older I get.

WIVES

A good wife and health
Are a man's best wealth.

A health to our widows. If they ever marry again may they do as
well!

Here's to the man who takes a wife,
Let him make no mistake:
For it makes a lot of difference
Whose wife it is you take.

Late last night I slew my wife,
Stretched her on the parquet flooring:
I was loath to take her life,
But I had to stop her snoring.

To our wives and sweethearts. May they never meet!

WOMAN AND WOMEN

Drink to fair woman, who, I think,
Is most entitled to it;
For if anything drives men to drink,
She certainly can do it.

Fill, fill, fill a brimming glass
Each man toast his favorite lass,
He who flinches is an ass,
Unworthy of love or wine.

Here's looking at you, dear!
Though I should pour a sea of wine,
My eyes would thirst for more.

Here's to God's first thought, "Man"!
Here's to God's second thought, "Woman"!
Second thoughts are always best,
So here's to Woman!

Here's to the gladness of her gladness when she's glad,
Here's to the sadness of her sadness when she's sad;
But the gladness of her gladness,
And the sadness of her sadness,
Are not in it with the madness of her madness when she's
mad.

Here's to the lasses we've loved, my lad,
Here's to the lips we've pressed;
For of kisses and lasses,

Like liquor in glasses,
The last is always the best.

I have never studied the art of paying compliments to women, but I must say that if all that has been said by orators and poets since the creation of the world in praise of women were applied to the women of America, it would not do them justice. God bless the women of America.

—ABRAHAM LINCOLN

Let her be clumsy, or let her be slim,
Young or ancient, I care not a feather;
So fill up a bumper, nay, fill to the brim,
Let us toast all the ladies together.

Of all your beauties, one by one,
I pledge, dear, I am thinking;
Before the tale were well begun
I had been dead of drinking.

They talk about a woman's sphere as though it had a limit;
There's not a place on earth or heaven,
There's not a task to mankind given,
There's not a blessing or a woe,
There's not a whispered yes or no,
There's not a life or birth,
That has a feather's weight of worth—
Without a woman in it.

To the ladies, God bless them,
May nothing distress them.

To the woman in her higher, nobler aspects, whether wife, widow, grass widow, mother-in-law, hired girl, telegraph operator, telephone helloer, queen, book agent, wet nurse, stepmother, boss, professional fat woman, professional double-headed woman, or professional beauty—God bless her.

—MARK TWAIN

'Tween woman and wine a man's lot is to smart,
For wine makes his head ache, and woman his heart.

We've toasted the mother and daughter
We've toasted the sweetheart and wife;
But somehow we missed her,
Our dear little sister—
The joy of another man's life.

What, sir, would people of the earth be without woman? They would be scarce, sir, almighty scarce.

—MARK TWAIN

A NOTE ON THE AUTHOR

PAUL DICKSON is the author of more than fifty books. He concentrates on writing about the American language, baseball, and twentieth-century history. He is a collector of words and wordplay whose other works of this nature include *Words*, *Names*, *Jokes*, *Slang*, *Family Words*, and *Words from the White House*, among others. He is a contributing editor for Dover Publications and *Washingtonian* magazine. His most recent books are *Bill Veeck: Baseball's Greatest Maverick* and *Authorisms: Words Wrought by Writers*. He lives in Maryland.